DISCOVER 🐾 DOGS WITH THE AMERICAN CANINE ASSOCIATION

ACA
AMERICAN CANINE ASSOCIATION INC.
OFFICIAL SEAL ®
America's Largest Veterinary
Health Tracking Canine
Registry

I LIKE
PORTUGUESE WATER DOGS!

Linda Bozzo

It is the mission of the American Canine Association (ACA) to provide registered dog owners with the educational support needed for raising, training, showing, and breeding the healthiest pets expected by responsible pet owners throughout the world. Through our activities and services, we encourage and support the dog world in order to promote best-known husbandry standards as well as to ensure that the voice and needs of our customers are quickly and properly addressed.

Our continued support, commitment, and direction are guided by our customers, including veterinary, legal, and legislative advisors. ACA aims to provide the most efficient, cooperative, and courteous service to our customers and strives to set the standard for education and problem solving for all who depend on our services.

For more information, please visit www.acacanines.com, email customerservice@acadogs.com, phone 1-800-651-8332, or write to the American Canine Association at PO Box 121107, Clermont, FL 34712.

Published in 2018 by Enslow Publishing, LLC.
101 W. 23rd Street, Suite 240, New York, NY 10011

Library of Congress Cataloging-in-Publication Data

Names: Bozzo, Linda, author.
Title: I like Portuguese water dogs! / Linda Bozzo.
Description: New York, NY : Enslow Publishing, 2018. | Series: Discover dogs with the American Canine Association | Includes bibliographical references and index. | Audience: Grades K to 3.
Identifiers: LCCN 2017013665| ISBN 9780766091177 (library bound) | ISBN 9780766091153 (pbk.) | ISBN 9780766091160 (6 pack)
Subjects: LCSH: Portuguese water dog—Juvenile literature.
Classification: LCC SF429.P87 B69 2017 | DDC 636.73—dc23
LC record available at https://lccn.loc.gov/2017013665

Printed in China

To Our Readers: We have done our best to make sure all websites in this book were active and appropriate when we went to press. However, the author and the publisher have no control over and assume no liability for the material available on those websites or on any websites they may link to. Any comments or suggestions can be sent by email to customerservice@enslow.com.

Photo Credits: Cover, p. 1 cynoclub/Shutterstock.com; p. 3 (left) © suefeldberg/iStock/Thinkstock; pp. 3 (right), 13 (left), 14, 19, 21 Courtesy Iwona Kossowski; p. 5 YAY Media AS/Alamy Stock Photo; p. 6 Julia Christe/Getty Images; pp. 9, 10 Rod Stables/EyeEm/Getty Images; p. 13 (collar) © graphicphoto/iStock/Thinkstock, (bed) Luisa Leal Photography/Shutterstock.com, (brush) In-Finity/Shutterstock.com, (food and water bowls) exopixel/Shutterstock.com, (leash, toys) © iStockphoto.com/Liliboas; p. 17 Saul Loeb/AFP/Getty Images; p. 18 © iStockphoto.com/sbrogan.

Enslow Publishing
101 W. 23rd Street
Suite 240
New York, NY 10011
USA
enslow.com

CONTENTS

IS A PORTUGUESE WATER DOG RIGHT FOR YOU?

Portuguese water dogs make excellent pets for **active** families. If you like being around water, the Portuguese water dog may be right for you.

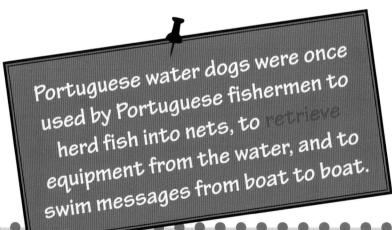

Portuguese water dogs were once used by Portuguese fishermen to herd fish into nets, to retrieve equipment from the water, and to swim messages from boat to boat.

A DOG OR A PUPPY?

Portuguese water dogs learn quickly. But training takes time. If you do not have time to train a puppy, you may want an older Portuguese water dog instead.

Portuguese water dogs are known to chew a lot as puppies.

LOVING YOUR PORTUGUESE WATER DOG

This dog is fun-loving and has lots of energy. She enjoys doing tasks and learning new things. Love your Portuguese water dog by taking her for a swim—her favorite thing to do!

EXERCISE

Portuguese water dogs enjoy long walks on a **leash**. Games, like **fetch**, will keep your dog happy. Swimming is great exercise for this breed.

Portuguese water dogs have a waterproof coat and webbed toes for swimming.

FEEDING YOUR PORTUGUESE WATER DOG

Portuguese water dogs can be fed wet or dry dog food. Ask a **veterinarian (vet)**, a doctor for animals, which food is best for your dog and how much to feed her.

Give your Portuguese water dog fresh, clean water every day.

Remember to keep your dog's food and water dishes clean. Dirty dishes can make a dog sick.

Do not feed your dog people food. It can make her sick.

Your new dog will need:

a collar with a tag

a bed

a brush

food and water dishes

a leash

toys

A Portuguese water dog's hair will keep on growing, so visits to the groomer are a must.

GROOMING

Portuguese water dogs **shed** little to none. This means little hair falls out or in some cases, no hair falls out at all. Your Portuguese water dog will need to be brushed often and bathed when needed. Use a shampoo made just for dogs.

A Portuguese water dog's nails will need to be clipped. A vet or **groomer** can show you how. Your dog's ears should be cleaned, and his teeth should be brushed by an adult.

WHAT YOU SHOULD KNOW

Portuguese water dogs make great walking and jogging buddies. If not exercised enough, Portuguese water dogs can get into trouble. They are good with children as well as with other pets.

You will need to take your new dog to the vet for a checkup. He will need shots, called vaccinations, and yearly checkups to keep him healthy. If you think your dog may be sick or hurt, call your vet.

A GOOD FRIEND

No matter which activity you choose, like a good friend, your Portuguese water dog will be by your side.

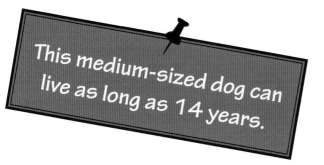
This medium-sized dog can live as long as 14 years.

NOTE TO PARENTS

It is important to consider having your dog spayed or neutered when the dog is young. Spaying and neutering are operations that prevent unwanted puppies and can help improve the overall health of your dog.

It is also a good idea to microchip your dog, in case he or she gets lost. A vet will implant a microchip under the skin containing an identification number that can be scanned at a vet's office or animal shelter. The microchip registry is contacted and the company uses the ID number to look up your information from a database.

Some towns require licenses for dogs, so be sure to check with your town clerk.

For more information, speak with a vet.

There are many dogs, young and old, waiting to be adopted from animal shelters and rescue groups.

active Always doing something.

fetch To go after a toy and bring it back.

groomer A person who bathes and brushes dogs.

leash A chain or strap that attaches to a dog's collar.

retrieve To bring back.

shed When dog hair falls out so new hair can grow.

vaccinations Shots that dogs need to stay healthy.

veterinarian (vet) A doctor for animals.

waterproof Not able to get wet.

Read About Dogs

Books

Carney, Elizabeth. *Woof! 100 Fun Facts About Dogs.* Washington, DC: National Geographic Children's Books, 2017.

Mair, Cole. *Dogs from Head to Tail.* New York, NY: Gareth Stevens Publishing, 2016.

Murray, Julie. *Dogs.* Minneapolis, MN: Abdo Kids, 2015.

Websites

American Canine Association Inc., Kids Corner
www.acakids.com
Visit the official website of the American Canine Association.

National Geographic for Kids, Pet Central
kids.nationalgeographic.com / explore / pet-central /
Learn more about dogs and other pets at the official site of the National Geographic Society for Kids.

INDEX